Amazing
Animals

Megan K. Wasp

Abrams
Learning Trends

Waterbury, CT
www.abramslearningtrends.com

Contents

Life in the wild isn't easy. Animals must hunt for prey or plants to eat. Predators hunt *them* for food. Animals sometimes face harsh weather.

Animals survive in amazing ways!

The Great Horned Owl uses *camouflage* to hide in the forest.

The owl's feathers match the colors in the forest.

Predators can't find the owl while it's sleeping. Can you?

What other animals might hide in this forest?

The Poison Arrow Frog isn't hiding! It has brightly colored skin to warn predators that it is poisonous.

What other animals have bright coloring to warn predators?

The cheetah uses speed to survive. It is so fast, it can outrun its prey.

What other animals use speed to catch prey?

The tortoise and the snail can't move fast.

They stay safe by hiding inside a shell.

What other animals hide inside a shell?

How does a skunk protect itself?

It sprays predators with a smelly liquid!

The octopus sprays something, too—black ink!

While the enemy can't see, the octopus disappears!

Watch how the puffer fish scares away predators!

It puffs itself up and sticks out its sharp spines!

The porcupine releases sharp spines called *quills*.

What other animals have sharp spines to protect themselves?

A thick fur coat protects the Arctic Fox from its enemy— the bitter cold winter!

What other animals grow thicker fur in the winter?

The Jackrabbit has to stay cool in the hot, dry desert. Body heat escapes through its very big ears.

What other animals use big ears to stay cool?

We saw lots of amazing animals!

How does each one survive?